HISTORY UNCUT

THE REAL
Anne Boleyn

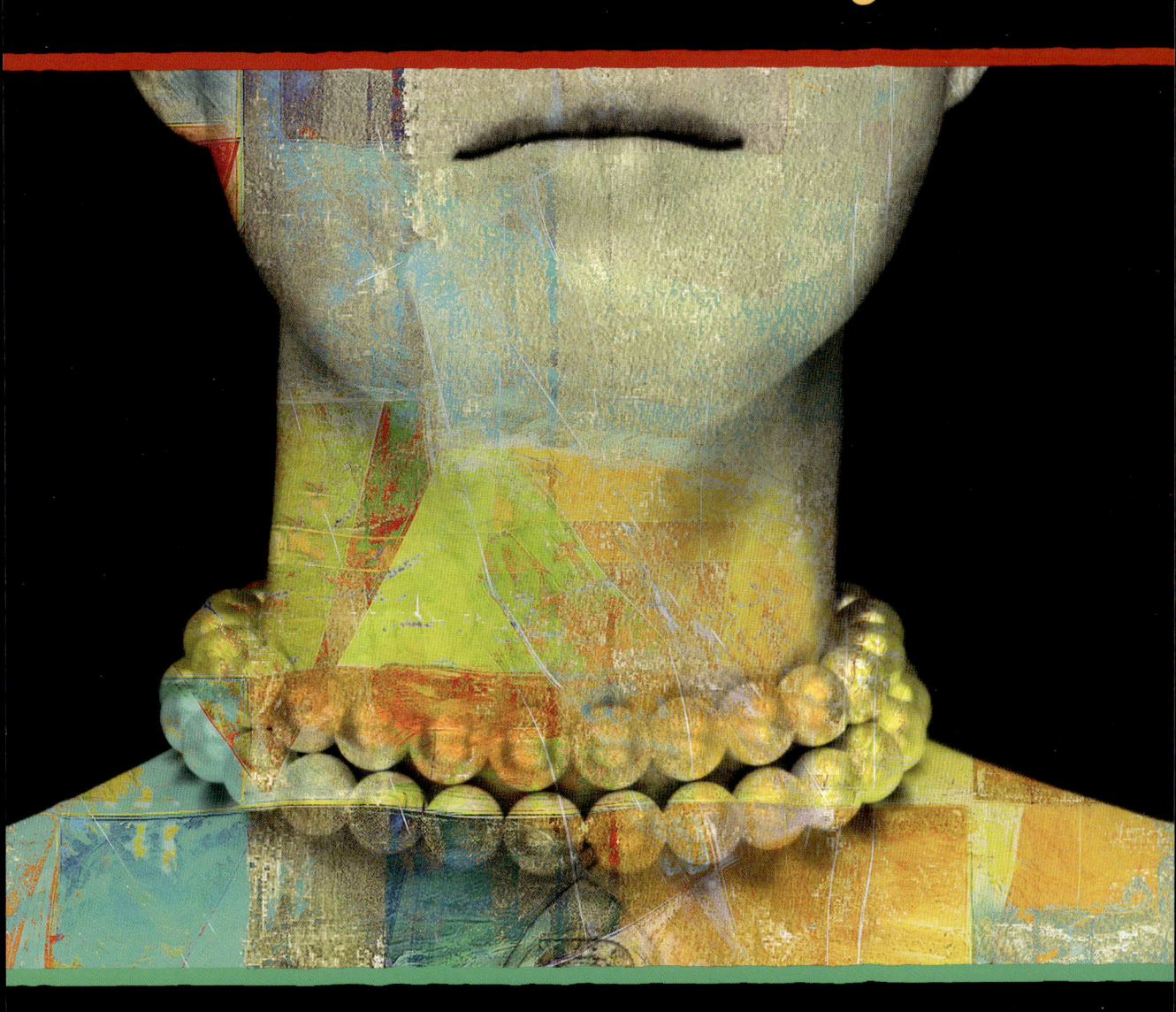

Virginia Loh-Hagan

45th Parallel Press

Published in the United States of America by Cherry Lake Publishing
Ann Arbor, Michigan
www.cherrylakepublishing.com

Reading Adviser: Marla Conn MS, Ed., Literacy specialist, Read-Ability, Inc.
Book Designer: Felicia Macheske

Photo Credits: © Karramba Production/Shutterstock.com, cover, 1; Unknown artist, Oil on panel attributed as Anne Boleyn, held at the National Portrait Gallery: NPG 668p, This work is in the public domain in the United States because it was published (or registered with the U.S. Copyright Office) before January 1, 1923., 5, 30; © Kiselev Andrey Valerevich/Shutterstock.com, 7; © DarkBird/Shutterstock.com, 9; © Thomas Barrat/Shutterstock.com, 11; © Piotr Piatrouski/Shutterstock.com, 12; © Georgios Kollidas/Shutterstock.com, 15; © Oleksandr Kolesnyk/Shutterstock.com, 17; Hans Holbein the Younger - Jane Seymour, Queen of England, Kunsthistorisches Museum, This work is in the public domain in the United States because it was published (or registered with the U.S. Copyright Office) before January 1, 1923., 19; © Shaiith/Shutterstock.com, 20; © Lia Koltyrina/Shutterstock.com, 23; © Spiroview Inc/Shutterstock.com, 24; © Kiselev Andrey Valerevich/Shutterstock.com 27; © Ipedan/Shutterstock.com, 29

Graphic Elements Throughout: © iulias/Shutterstock.com; © Thinglass/Shutterstock.com; © kzww/Shutterstock.com; © A_Lesik/Shutterstock.com; © MegaShabanov/Shutterstock.com; © Groundback Atelier/Shutterstock.com; © saki80/Shutterstock.com

Copyright © 2019 by Cherry Lake Publishing
All rights reserved. No part of this book may be reproduced or utilized in any form or by any means without written permission from the publisher.

45th Parallel Press is an imprint of Cherry Lake Publishing.

Library of Congress Cataloging-in-Publication Data

Names: Loh-Hagan, Virginia.
Title: Anne Boleyn / by Virginia Loh-Hagan.
Description: Ann Arbor : Cherry Lake, 2018. | Series: History uncut | Includes bibliographical references and index.
Identifiers: LCCN 2018004550 | ISBN 9781534129498 (hardcover) | ISBN 9781534131194 (pdf) | ISBN 9781534132696 (pbk.) | ISBN 9781534134393 (hosted ebook)
Subjects: LCSH: Anne Boleyn, Queen, consort of Henry VIII, King of England, 1507-1536--Juvenile literature. | Queens--England--Biography--Juvenile literature. | Great Britain--History--Henry VIII, 1509-1547--Juvenile literature.
Classification: LCC DA333.B6 L64 2018 | DDC 942.05/2092 [B] --dc23
LC record available at https://lccn.loc.gov/2018004550

Cherry Lake Publishing would like to acknowledge the work of The Partnership for 21st Century Skills. Please visit www.p21.org for more information.

Printed in the United States of America
Corporate Graphics

Table of Contents

Chapter 1
Anne Boleyn
The Story You Know 4

Chapter 2
A French Education 6

Chapter 3
Out with the Old 10

Chapter 4
Useless Girls?! 14

Chapter 5
To the Tower! 18

Chapter 6
Wicked Witch 22

Chapter 7
Off with Her Head 26

Timeline 30

Consider This! 31
Learn More 31
Glossary 32
Index 32
About the Author 32

CHAPTER 1

Anne Boleyn
The Story You Know

Anne Boleyn was Queen of England. Then, she was **beheaded**. This means her head was chopped off.

She was King Henry VIII's second wife. She helped start the English **Reformation**. Reformation means a change. Reform means to make something better.

During her life, men were in charge. They made all the rules. Boleyn was different from other women. She was smart. She was clever. She was brave. She was lively. She did well in a man's world. She used her education. She used her style. She used her influence. She paved the way for women in politics. But there's more to her story…

King Henry VIII had 6 wives.

CHAPTER 2

A French Education

Boleyn was born in 1501. She was born in England. She was born to a **noble** family. Noble means high class.

She wanted to rise in her class rank. She wanted more power. She wanted more education. She was sent **abroad**. Abroad means overseas. First, she studied under Margaret of Austria. She learned math, reading, writing, and history. She learned good manners. Then, she was sent to France. She served in royal courts. She learned from queens. She read books. She studied many topics. She learned French. She learned to dance. She learned to sing. She learned to sew. She learned to play games. She learned to ride horses. She learned art.

Boleyn was of more noble birth than King Henry VIII's future wives.

SETTING THE WORLD STAGE
1501

- Michelangelo was a famous artist. He was from Italy. He was 26 years old in 1501. He started sculpting *David*. This is his most famous piece. It's made from a single piece of white marble. It's 17 feet (5 meters) tall. It's over 12,000 pounds (5,443 kilograms).

- Catherine of Aragon was a princess of Spain. In 1501, she was 15 years old. She left Spain. She traveled to London. She traveled over 500 miles (805 kilometers) on horseback. She married Arthur Tudor. Arthur was King Henry VIII's older brother. He was next in line to the English throne. He died in 1502. Then, Catherine married King Henry VIII.

- Amerigo Vespucci was an Italian explorer. He sailed to the New World. In 1501, he sailed to Brazil. He discovered and named All Saints' Bay. It's the largest bay in Brazil. Vespucci was the first European to visit the bay. He saw it on his second trip to the Americas.

"By daily proof you shall me find to be to you both loving and kind." – Anne Boleyn

She trained to be a good wife. But she also trained to be a good partner. She learned new ways of thinking. She met Marguerite of Navarre. Marguerite was the French king's sister. She was a reformer. Boleyn learned about different religions.

Boleyn was influenced by the French court. She took on French styles. She took on French ways. Strong French women were her role models. They had minds of their own. They formed their own ideas. They ruled. They made decisions.

Boleyn also learned about courtly love. She learned how to impress men. She learned how to talk to men. She learned how to get men to admire her.

The French were more liberal than the English.

CHAPTER 3

Out with the Old

Boleyn returned to England. She became a lady in Queen Catherine's court. Queen Catherine of Aragon was King Henry VIII's first wife.

Boleyn was different. She didn't act like other ladies. She made her own rules. She was stylish. She laughed loudly. She liked arguing. She was charming. People liked her.

King Henry VIII fell in love with her. He wanted to marry her. But he and his wife were Catholics. Catholics weren't allowed to divorce.

Boleyn read a book by William Tyndale. She showed it to the king. This book said kings answered to God, not the pope. This inspired King Henry VIII.

The Canterbury Cathedral became headquarters for the Church of England.

He formed the Church of England. He became its leader. He divorced Catherine. He married Boleyn. Boleyn supported the new religion. She read the Bible in English. She shared Bibles with others. She hired strong leaders. She protected people.

King Henry VIII made her the **Marquess** of Pembroke. This is a high position in court. It's meant for a man. This made Boleyn a **peer**. She was equal to other nobles. She was noble in her own right. She wasn't just noble because of her father. She wasn't just noble because of her husband. She was above most male lords. She could do business with them. She ruled with King Henry VIII.

Boleyn built partnerships with other countries.

All in the Family

Mary Boleyn was born in 1500. She was Anne Boleyn's sister. People said she was prettier. (But Anne was smarter.) She was the oldest child. She was educated in France. She was a lover of the French king. She returned to England. She became a lover of King Henry VIII. Some people think she had two of his children. She married twice. In 1520, she married for duty. She married William Carey. Carey was rich. He was one of King Henry VIII's advisors. He died of the sweating sickness. In 1534, she married for love. She married in secret. She married William Stafford. Stafford was a soldier. He was poor. He was below Mary Boleyn's class. This made the king and queen mad. They banned Mary from court. She died in 1543.

"Remember me when you do pray, that hope doth lead from day to day." —Anne Boleyn

CHAPTER 4

Useless Girls?!

King Henry VIII and Queen Catherine had a daughter. That's another reason why the king divorced her. He wanted sons. He needed male **heirs**. Heirs have legal claims. They can inherit the throne.

King Henry VIII thought Boleyn would give him a son. Many predicted a boy. The French king was asked to be the godfather. Parties were planned.

Boleyn had a baby in 1533. But the baby wasn't a boy. It was a girl. The girl's name was Elizabeth I. She was named after both grandmothers. The king was sad. He wanted a son. But Boleyn didn't have any other children. So, King Henry VIII stopped loving her. People said girls were "useless." They turned against Boleyn.

King Henry VIII's first daughter was named Mary.

15

THAT Happened?!?

Many think Anne Boleyn's ghost lives on. Her spirit is restless. Some think she died a wrongful death. This means she was killed unfairly. Her ghost is seen on May 19. It shows up every year. It shows up at Blickling Hall. This is where she may have been born. Her ghost rides in a carriage. Six horses pull the carriage. The horses don't have heads. A headless horseman drives the carriage. Her ghost doesn't have a head. It holds her head on her lap. It reaches the Blickling Hall. Some say her ghost walks into the house. It holds her head. It walks around the house. Then, it vanishes into thin air when the sun rises. People say her ghost haunts several places. It haunts Hever Castle. This is where she grew up. Her ghost also haunts the Tower of London. This is where she died.

"But even if I were to suffer a thousand deaths, my love for you will not abate one jot." — Anne Boleyn

Boleyn's daughter turned out to be very useful. Elizabeth was 2 years old when Boleyn died. Elizabeth I took power at age 25. She became a great queen. She ruled for 44 years. She brought peace. She beat the French. She beat the Spanish. She promoted the arts. She promoted her mother's religion. Her reign was known as the Golden Age. She wore a special ring. The ring was taken from her body. It was sent to the next king. It was proof of her death. The ring had a picture of Boleyn. Elizabeth had her mother's **ambitions** and her father's strength. Ambitions are goals.

Boleyn's greatest contribution to England was Elizabeth I.

CHAPTER 5

To the Tower

Boleyn became powerful. She gained fans. But she also gained **foes**. Foes are enemies. Boleyn argued with the king's advisors. Some thought she was stepping out of her place. They didn't like strong women.

King Henry VIII wanted to marry Jane Seymour. Seymour was the opposite of Boleyn. She was meek. She obeyed. She didn't argue. King Henry VIII needed to get rid of Boleyn. His advisors helped him. They investigated Boleyn. They accused her of high **treason**. Treason means betrayal. People said she cheated on the king. They said she tried to kill the king.

King Henry VIII said Seymour was his favorite wife.

Boleyn was **arrested**. Arrest means to take to jail. Boleyn was sent to the Tower of London. She was in the Tower twice. She was there when she was waiting to be crowned. And she was there as a prisoner.

Boleyn was tried before a **jury**. A jury is a group of peers. They decide if someone is guilty or not. People spoke against Boleyn. The king and his advisors may have forced people to say bad things about her. They wanted Boleyn out of the way.

The case against Boleyn was weak. There was no real proof. Boleyn denied everything. But it didn't matter. Boleyn was found guilty.

In prison, Boleyn cried. She asked for her family. She asked what she did wrong. She wrote to the king.

Bad Blood

Thomas Cromwell was born in 1485. He was King Henry VIII's chief adviser. He was a lawyer. He was a statesman. He helped the king marry Boleyn. Both Cromwell and Boleyn believed in the new religion. They wanted reform. They wanted change. But they disagreed on many other things. Cromwell wanted the king to get rid of the old churches. Boleyn disagreed. She wanted people to stop believing in the old religion. But she didn't want to destroy it. She knew the old churches helped people. She knew they helped the poor. She accused Cromwell of giving the king bad advice. This made Cromwell mad. The king fell in love with someone else. He wanted to get rid of Boleyn. Cromwell helped him. He spied on Boleyn. He got people to tell stories about her. He set up her death.

"The executioner is, I believe, very expert. And, my neck is very slender." — Anne Boleyn

CHAPTER 6

Wicked Witch

Some people thought Boleyn was a witch. People questioned the king. They questioned why he left Queen Catherine. They questioned why he left the Catholic Church. They blamed the devil. They blamed Boleyn.

Boleyn looked like everyone else. She didn't look special. But she was special. She was witty. She had a lot of energy. She charmed people. Some people wondered how Boleyn got the king's love. They thought she was a witch. They thought she used magic to control him.

King Charles V of Spain called Boleyn a witch.

24

Some people thought Boleyn had 6 fingers. The sixth finger was on her right hand. This added to the stories about her being a witch. Any **deformities** were seen as signs of evil. Deformities are flaws. Nicholas Sander was a Catholic. He wrote about Boleyn's sixth finger. He was the first to do so.

People also said she had moles. They said she had a chin wart. They said she had an odd tooth. The tooth stuck out. It stuck out of her upper lip. But these were all rumors.

◀ If Boleyn had had any deformities, the king wouldn't have married her.

CHAPTER 7

Off with Her Head

Boleyn was one of the smartest English queens. This gave her great power. But her power led to her death. Some people were scared of smart women. They wanted her gone. Boleyn was to be burned alive. Burning is a painful way to die. King Henry VIII stepped in. He ordered a beheading instead.

Common people got axed. Queens shouldn't be killed by axes. So, King Henry VIII ordered a special sword. The sword was from France. He also paid for an expert swordsman. Boleyn was the first English queen to be publicly **executed**. Execute means to kill.

The jury sentenced Boleyn to death.

Explained by
SCIENCE

Polydactyl means having many digits. Digits are toes or fingers. Some animals have more digits than normal. Some humans do, too. This is due to mutations. Mutations are changes. They're changes from what's normal. They mean something is wrong with genes. Genes decide how people look. Some people are born with extra digits. This can happen on one hand or one foot. This can happen on both hands or feet. This can happen on one hand and one foot. These extra digits are smaller. They're not formed all the way. They're made of skin, tissue, or bones. Skin can be removed. It's harder to remove bones. About one in every 500 humans has extra digits.

On May 19, 1536, Boleyn was scheduled to die. She said, "I have not come here to preach a **sermon**. I have come here to die." A sermon is a speech. Boleyn wore a gray dress. She tucked in her hair. She said good-bye to her ladies. She asked for prayers. She knelt. She whispered her final prayers. She didn't cry. The sword hit her neck. It only took a single strike. Boleyn's death was quick.

Her ladies picked up her body and head. They wrapped them in white cloth. They placed them in a chest. Boleyn was buried by the Tower. Her grave was unmarked. But her life wasn't unmarked. Boleyn was a woman before her time.

Boleyn praised King Henry VIII before she died.

Timeline

1501 Boleyn was born. Her exact birthday is unknown. There were no church records.

1513 Boleyn was sent overseas. She studied under Margaret of Austria. Margaret ruled over the Netherlands. She said Boleyn was "so bright and so pleasant."

1515 Boleyn was sent to France. She was a lady-in-waiting for Queen Mary and Queen Claude.

1521 Boleyn returned to England. She planned to marry James Butler. This would make her an Irish countess. That marriage was stopped.

1522 Boleyn met King Henry VIII. She was in a dance. She played "Perseverance." She wore a white dress. The dress had gold thread.

1526 Boleyn and King Henry VIII wrote love letters.

1528 Boleyn got the sweating sickness. She got better. Others died.

1533 Boleyn married King Henry VIII. They had 2 weddings. They had a secret wedding. Then, they had a public wedding.

1533 Boleyn became Queen. She wore St. Edward's Crown. This crown was special. It was for born rulers only. Boleyn was the wife of a ruler. It was unusual for her to wear it.

1533 Boleyn gave birth to Elizabeth I. Elizabeth I had red hair.

1536 Boleyn got jealous of King Henry VIII and Jane Seymour. The king gave Seymour a necklace. The necklace had his picture. Boleyn saw it. She grabbed it. She hurt her hand.

1536 Boleyn was taken to the Tower of London.

1536 Boleyn was beheaded. She was treated like a traitor to the Crown.

Consider This!

Take a Position! King Henry VIII did a lot to marry Boleyn. He got divorced. He left the church. He ignored his friends. Was it worth it? Should he have married Boleyn or not? Argue your point with reasons and evidence.

Say What? Learn more about England in the 1500s. Learn more about women's roles. Anne Boleyn was different from others. Explain how.

Think About It! Prince Harry and Meghan Markle are engaged. They decided to marry on May 19. Boleyn died on May 19. What are the connections? What does this mean? Do you believe in fate?

Learn More

Egan, Pamela. *Kings and Queens of England and Scotland*. New York: Shelter Harbor Press, 2017.

Labrecque, Ellen, and Jake Murray (illust.). *Who Was Henry VIII?* New York: Penguin Workshop, 2018.

Meyer, Carolyn. *Doomed Queen Anne*. San Diego: Harcourt, 2002.

Glossary

abroad (uh-BRAWD) overseas

ambitions (am-BISH-uhnz) goals; desires

arrested (uh-REST-id) taken to jail

beheaded (bih-HED-id) had one's head chopped off

deformities (dih-FORM-ih-teez) flaws or abnormalities

executed (EK-suh-kyoot-ed) killed

foes (FOHZ) enemies

heirs (AIRZ) children who have legal claims to inheritance

jury (JOOR-ee) group of peers

marquess (MAR-kwess) a noble title below duke and higher than earl

noble (NOH-buhl) high class

peer (PEER) of the same class, equal

reformation (reh-for-MAY-shuhn) change; improvement

sermon (SUR-muhn) speech especially for a church event

treason (TREE-zuhn) betrayal

Index

beheaded, 4, 26, 30

executed, 26

Catherine of Aragon, 8, 10, 12, 14, 22

Elizabeth I, 14, 17, 30

England (English), 4, 6, 8, 9, 10, 11, 12, 13, 17, 26, 30, 31

England (English) (*cont.*)
  Church of, 12

France (French), 6, 9, 13, 14, 17, 26, 30

King Henry VIII, 4, 5, 7, 8, 10, 12–15, 18, 19, 21, 26, 29–31

Reformation, 4, 9, 21

Seymour, Jane, 18, 19, 30

Spain (Spanish), 8, 17, 23

treason, 18

Vespucci, Amerigo, 8

About the Author

Dr. Virginia Loh-Hagan is an author, university professor, former classroom teacher, and curriculum designer. She loves learning about British history. She lives in San Diego with her very tall husband and very naughty dogs. To learn more about her, visit www.virginialoh.com.